Mollie,
thank you for
coming out
tonight!
4/17/08

"It has been incredible to see God use Bradley Hathaway's writing to encourage, convict, and strengthen so many people."

–Jason Dunn
Facedown Records and
No Innocent Victim

"This guy is good, I mean real good ...
I am talking really, really good."

–Josh Scogin
The Chariot

"A highly entertaining and slightly unnerving exercise in honesty and spiritual insight. Well worth the read or listen."

–Josh Childers
The Showdown

"Bradley Hathaway is the poetic voice of the mosh pit. His relevance to the hardest of the hardcore, especially those with their arms crossed standing in the back, is creatively and simplistically brought to life for those who think they're too 'scene' to read poetry."

–Brad Moist
A&R, General Manager,
Mono Vs Stereo

"Bradley is a breath of fresh air when he performs. His brutal honesty and tongue-in-cheek banter make for thought-provoking dicussions after shows. I may not agree with some of the topics, but I know this kid has heart and it's in the right place."

–Peter Kowalsky
Remembering Never

"Bradley uses satirical wit to convey a simplistic passion for a world filled with beauty. There is a big picture, and he is seeing it for what it is somewhere past the self-defeating and often amusing trappings of human nature. Respect the freakin' poet."

–Josh Dies
Showbread

"I do not believe in Bradley's version of the Almighty. I do not subscribe to the Christian worldview at all, actually. I think that Bradley's live show is irritating. I think that Bradley probably just needs a girlfriend. Having said all of that, he is something of a gem. It's all in there somewhere—joy, pain, irony, humility, arrogance. All packed into a tiny frame with a voice like a megaphone and an infectious energy that provokes you just enough to demand your full attention. He offers himself in word as he does in person ... as an exercise in contradictions."

–Matthew Putman
Lovedrug

"Bradley's poetry has encouraged me in my faith, and his brutal honesty has challenged me to evaluate things in my own life."

–Kevin Kiehn
The Wedding

ALL THE HITS SO FAR

BUT DON'T EXPECT TOO MUCH

BRADLEY
HATHAWAY

[RELEVANTBOOKS]

Published by Relevant Books
A division of Relevant Media Group, Inc.

www.relevantbooks.com
www.relevantmediagroup.com

Design by Relevant Solutions
Cover design by Joshua Smith
Interior design by Jeremy Kennedy
Bradley Hathaway photographs by Azuree Norman

Library of Congress Control Number: 2005928894
International Standard Book Number: 0-9763642-3-9

For information or bulk orders:
RELEVANT MEDIA GROUP, INC.
100 SOUTH LAKE DESTINY DR. STE. 200
ORLANDO, FL 32810
407-660-1411

www.thebradley.net

06 07 08 9 8 7 6 5 4 3

Printed in the United States of America

FOR THE ONES
I love very much

CON

Poetry, Prose & Other Sundry Items

FOREWORD

BURN IT DOWN AND WALK AWAY

The flames rose up as we watched our past turn to dust. A ringing blasted in our ears from the farewell concert the night before. We knew The Gate was gone forever. What next? Burn it down and walk away.

Bradley and I stood outside in the hot July Arkansas sun saying goodbye to the thing that we knew best. Before Bradley Hathaway was known across the globe as a long-haired storytelling poet, he ran a music venue called The Gate, in the small town of Fort Smith, Arkansas. I first came to The Gate as an intimidated junior high kid with my band's first demo tape in hand, trying to score our first gig. I walked into the dark brick room, which always had a leak and terrible sound, as a hardcore band was playing something close to music. I came from another world. Rock 'n' roll was where I lived and what my band, The Exception, played, but since this was the only venue in town, I had to take what I could get. After seeing the place, I expected Bradley to be an evil gothic figure, someone you wouldn't want to meet alone in a dark alley. Fate can be tricky. Instead, I found a sissy white boy, who was twenty but looked about twelve, grinning from ear to ear, dancing alone under a flashing "Millennium Ball." I had my doubts about him, yet after a few years of constant shows with The Exception and occasionally working the soundboard at The Gate, a friendship developed.

When I first met Bradley, he was the man who held the strings in the local music scene, but as God would have it, one day the string started to stretch. Bradley's first poem ... a slight tug on the string. His first performance of poetry ... the string tears. The world outside was calling for him. Bradley's first tour in the summer of 2004 ... the string breaks. Two years after we met, Bradley left on his debut American tour: I was about to enter the twelfth grade, my last year at home before I, too, would step out into the big world. We had no idea what God had in store. (We still don't, in all truth.)

Bradley's first show on his first tour—telling hardcore kids about his manhood, sex, and hugs—was in Tulsa, Oklahoma, where fifteen crusty skater kids heckled him from the side of the stage. Over the

phone that night, Bradley spoke in a voice mixed with excitement and self-doubt. "This is great, but what will people think of poetry at a rock show?" I assured him that it was okay and that God would not let him get killed by the kids of Syracuse (although I heard he almost got roughed up in Flint). Then four weeks later, Bradley called me from the Cornerstone Festival in Illinois. "Dude, I got on stage before Blindside and rocked it in front of nearly 10,000 people!" I smiled. The Exception played for twelve people in a heavy metal bar in Little Rock that same night. Sometimes life isn't fair.

It is now May of 2005. Summer is fast approaching the Arkansas River Valley, and Bradley has just spent four hours on the computer in my house trying to book flights to Europe. The Exception is releasing our first full-length record and going on our first U.S. tour, which could fall apart at any minute, while Bradley debates whether he should stay five or seven days in Iceland during the European leg of his upcoming world tour. Life still isn't fair. He is going to share his deep revelations about "fat women" and "joy" with people all over the world. The Lord picks funny people to be His messengers. The fire is still burning bright.

Bradley changed my life and, from what I see on MySpace, many of your lives, too. He is a voice crying out in the wilderness, speaking the truth that we all know but are too afraid to hear. Bradley is not a prophet, and he is not a priest. He is a dude who eats my food and runs up my cell phone bill, yet God has used him as an incredible tool to spread His word. God manifests Himself in strange places. Sometimes it is in the stained glass of a cathedral, and sometimes

on a crusty couch on the wrong side of the tracks in small-town Arkansas, waiting for the next big thing to happen.

The sun beat down on our faces as Bradley and I sat on a couch outside of The Gate. After closing the venue down, we had to do something with its smelly, beat-up furniture. Instead of taking it to the dump, we decided to put it on the sidewalk with a "free" sign next to it. We plopped down on the couch to see what would happen. Not five minutes later, a woman with six kids pulled up in a broken-down Chevy van and asked if we were giving away the couch. Bradley said, "Yes, and we'll even deliver it for you." So we hopped into his 1988 Ford pick-up truck and followed the van, giving away the last remains of The Gate. Bradley showed me how to fan the all-consuming fire of grace. Burn it down and walk away.

What will happen in the next few years? When will Bradley look at this book and say, "Burn it down and walk away"? Only God knows, but do not fret when that day comes (and it certainly will), because Bradley is a gift. We should enjoy the gift but love the Giver. Let the words from these pages be a gift to you. Listen for the voice beyond the pretty eyelashes, hardcore T-shirts, and girl jeans to find the fire that is inside of you. Then take a deep breath. Take one last drink. Shout to the wind. Burn it down and walk away.

John Gladwin
Bradley's Friend

ACKNOW-LEDGMENTS

I have been blessed this past year to travel all over the United States and parts of Canada reciting poetry. During this time I have met and spent time with some of the most amazing people I have ever been around. From a mom in Nashville, Tennessee, making me granola and yogurt with a note that says "made with a mother's love" to sharing communion with Texas toast and water in Atlanta with twenty-something strangers or hanging out with a family in their ice cream shop in Porterville, California. So many wonderful happenings and so many wonderful people! And so many times have I hurt people. Said stupid things. Acted uninterested. Been ungrateful. Came off like a rock star instead of a servant. To those

I have hurt, I am sorry. I am sorry for taking you, and what I have been given, for granted. While I haven't always showed my appreciation or sincerity for what many of you have shown me, please know that I am very thankful.

A list of thanks would be far too long, so instead I say thank you to every band that has taken me on tour or played/peformed with me, every promoter who has put on a show for me, every kid who has emailed me telling me his or her story and how I have played a part in it, everyone who has prayed for me, everyone who has let me stay at their house and eat their food, everyone who has bought my merchandise, everyone who has given me money to get from city to city, everyone who listened as they saw me perform, every smile on your faces, every kid who sings along, and my friends and family who continue to hold me accountable with their honesty and genuine love. Love, love, love to all of you in Jesus' name, Amen.

NTRO-
DUCTION

So I was thinking of writing about what most introductions are usually like, and then I was going to tell how mine is going to be different than the norm. But I can't think of what's supposed to be in an introduction. The publisher didn't even ask for one, but a few minutes ago I asked them about it, and they said, "Sure, write one." And now I don't even know what's supposed to be in one.

The only introduction that I can recall is C.S. Lewis' *Mere Christianity* where he explained why the book was written and where it came from. Maybe that's what an introduction is, but I did that for each of the poems, so I can't really do that here. At the moment,

I think it's funny that I'm mentioning C.S. Lewis. What book written by a Christian hasn't mentioned Lewis at some point? So I'm already hopping on the Clives Staples bandwagon, and everyone who is well read will be impressed and think, "Oh, he reads Lewis, so I can at least give him a chance because anyone who reads Lewis deserves at least a fair chance." Others of you are wondering who the heck Clives Staples is. Moving on ...

I thought about writing books when I was younger, and I always thought it was going to happen someday in my life, but not so soon and most definitely not a book of poetry. I was going to school for philosophy, and then on to seminary to learn the deep truths and mysteries of the Christian faith; surely books would be written along those lines, not about poetry.

But here I am, days away from this project being sent to the press to be mass produced and sold all over the world. Today is Wednesday, June 8, 2005, 2:51 in the afternoon. I'm wearing my polar bear pajama pants that my mom bought me. When she does buy me something, it's always stuff I don't need—like more pajama pants—and I get mad at her because I seriously only need one pair of pajama pants. I have no shirt on, and I look down to see chest hair numerous enough to still be counted by someone who cannot count past the teens yet. I'm eating crackers. I didn't eat breakfast, and I've not eaten lunch. I don't want to eat either, because I'm not even hungry. I'm depressed, really.

Yesterday I broke it off with my girl because I felt like God wouldn't have us together at this time and maybe not ever. This is coming from a dude who swore to never break it off with a girl for such a cop-out lame excuse given by Christian kids too afraid to say how they really feel and hide behind God. They're manipulating another by blaming it all on the good, all-knowing sweet Lord and Savior who has broken more boys' and girls' hearts than any pimp or playa can ever lay claim to. So I feel shady and confused, but I'm trusting that maybe she will be given back to me as Isaac was to Abraham. I don't know, though, maybe she won't.

Maybe I'm supposed to remain single, living the romantic ideal of a loner traveling about in the world, experiencing all the world has to offer, and being deep and thoughtful enough to write and let everyone else know what he has seen, what he believes, and blah blah blah. With my heart on my sleeve, I go and I write and I tell, and all is fine and dandy for the time being. I'm just twenty-three, but I don't know about being thirty-three and doing the same thing, let alone forty-three. Oh my goodness, and to think about being fifty-three and doing the same thing. For some reason I think I'm going to die young, in the next two years actually. No reason to think that, except I have a hunch about it, as funny as it sounds. I don't know, man. I don't even know what I'm saying "I don't know" to. I just don't know.

Here is much of who I am on paper. Things I've experienced or things I hope to experience or thoughts on things I think about. It's an awful responsibility that I've been thinking about the past couple days and couple weeks. I guess since I realized that this was for real: that I really am going to be writing a book, people really are going to read it, and people really are going to think it was great or it sucked. And the fear of all that has gotten me a bit intimidated. (I just used "intimidated" because I was too scared to say "afraid," by the way.) For all the boldness and truthfulness that everyone says I have, I'm quite afraid of being misunderstood or misrepresented. Sure I have said much of what I was thinking about most of the poems in here, but it's still so incomplete. Most likely you will never know me, will never have a conversation with me, and will never get to know me or my character beyond what you have read or heard about me, maybe from others or even maybe from myself. This makes for a weird feeling and thought.

Maybe I'm taking it too serious and overanalyzing it like a confusing text message. Once again, I just don't know. And that's what I keep coming back to: I don't know. I'm just a person. I'm a human being with no more right to say this or that about God or life or love than the next. I've just been given a talent to express it a bit more lovely than most people, but the fact that much of what I say resonates so well with so many people shows that I'm saying nothing new or special, just what is. Some, including myself, would argue that my talent isn't all it's cracked up to be. And thinking about some of my commentary in this book makes me cringe because I didn't know what to say about such and such, or even after I said it, I didn't like the way I said it. So I resign to not take myself too seriously. To just let what is written remain so. I didn't want to have a picture of myself in this book or even on the cover, but it is, so just let it be. It doesn't really matter in the end anyway. Yeah, I'll be misunderstood, and people will think this or that, but who cares. I have done my best and tried to represent what I believe with the utmost honor and integrity. Maybe one day, like Saint Augustine, I will later publish a book of retractions saying what I believed at twenty-three was wrong because maybe I am wrong here and there. I don't know.

But I know that I'm excited about this project, and in the next few minutes I will send this off, and the final piece of the book will be put in place, and I'll not be able to change anything. This year I will get to travel the world, make new friends, see new places, have new happenings, and eat more burritos. I can't begin to project how big this book will even get. Maybe it will get big enough, though, that I can actually have my own place to call home instead of my van Lil' Bean. Maybe I can take my books out of my friend's closet and set them up somewhere in a place that I have to come to after another tour is complete. Maybe it will be as surprisingly popular as *Napoleon Dynamite*. Maybe the Lord will use this book and me to change the lives of thousands of people. Millions of people even. Maybe I'll do for my generation what Jack Kerouac did for his, only a bit differently. Maybe it will totally flop and be out of print as soon as the first press runs out. I don't know. But until then, here is my first published book and a nice little CD to go with it. I hope you enjoy it, but if you don't, I think that is okay too.

NO
WORRIES
I'M GOING
TO...

WAIT,
WAIT,
WAIT!

WAIT a minute!
Hold up!

THE
PRESS!

I woke up today
without that

FIVE
MILLION POUND
BOULDER

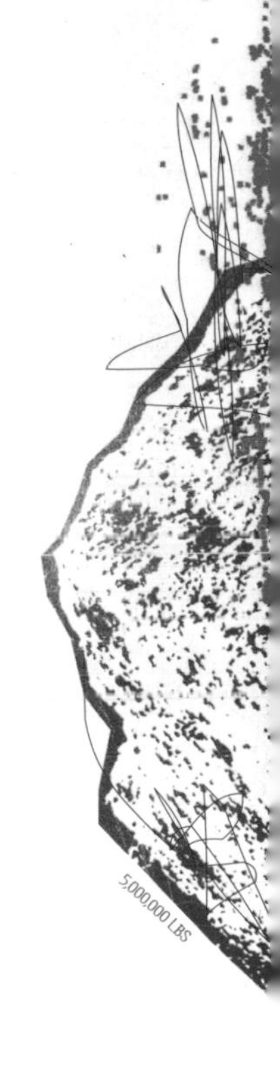

of StReSS
on my chest
And now
I feel BLESSED
And can rest

Oh! To REST these weary extremities
That have been INFLICTED with INFIRMITIES

Unseen or EXPERIENCED
by them before

SO TELL ME
What does the future
have in store?

(I don't know.)

But I'm just going to let TODAY
be today.

I'm going to WAKE up this morning
with a smile on my face
Look in the mirror
BRUSH my teeth
and NOT
WRACK
my BRAIN

Wondering if she's going to CALL me or not
Because when a girl says

"let's just be friends"

What she really means is:
"I'M NEVER GOING TO TALK TO YOU AGAIN"

ACCEPT it.

MOVE ON.

I just DID.

And AFTER that
I'm going to put on my play clothes
Go in the front yard
and climb that pecan tree
like I did LAST WEEK
BUT THIS TIME
Im not going to get halfway up there
and start debating
whether morality is:

A social adaptation.
A product of evolution.
Or put there by God.

I'm JUST going to climb the thing
and have fun like I did when I was a kid.

And after that I'm going to go to
VERTEBRATE zoology class
And listen to my
BORING
lifeless
instructor
talk about how
there are over fifty different species
of minnows
in just Arkansas alone.

But I'll smile.
Nod.

SHOW INTEREST.

Act interested.
Because that really is interesting
if you think about it...

NO WORRIES ...

And then after that
I'll go home
and have lunch.

The SAME ol' lunch again!
Two more
FRICKIN'
FROZEN
El Monterey Jack
BEAN and cheese burritos
With a glass
ofDISTILLED water
and an ORANGE.

But I'll give thanks
that I do have food to eat
because so many people don't.

And then after that
I'll go to work and paint.
~~BUT I'M NOT GOING~~
TO PAINT THAT
boring
EGGshell
white
On that old lady's wall
like she requested!

No...
NOT going to do it.

I'm going to pretend that I'm
a juvenile Leonardo
da Vinci
and paint a stick
FIGURE masterpiece
of a young couple frolicking
in a FIELD of FLOWERS
with little BUTTERFLIES
and gophers popping up
here
and there.

(I'm sure the old lady will appreciate it
later in life.)

And after that
I'm going to go have dinner with my Paw Paw.
And when he cries to me
about how his arthritis
is BAD.

His own daughter rejects him
HE'S SAD.

I'LL PUT MY ARM AROUND HIM
AND LISTEN.

Watch his
old
WEARY
eyes
glisten

As he experiences
my love for him.

NO WORRIES ...

~~And then after that~~
I'll go home

Sit on the FLOOR
And START
singing songs
to the ONE
who gave me
THIS JOY
that I'm feeling

But it's MORE
than just some
FLEETING feeling
It's eternal
truth
in which
I am reeling

~~And then at night~~
I'll lay my head
to rest
without the slightest bit
~~of fright~~
~~or fret~~
Knowing I made the day
the best I could

And that God
TRULY IS GOOD.

NO WORRIES, I'M GOING TO...

CONCERNING "NO WORRIES, I'M GOING TO ..."

I can't say that I'm crazy about this poem anymore, especially with it being the opener for this record and this book. Still, it has its purpose and shows where I was at when it was written. This was basically my average day two years ago. Now my days are hardly normal, but back then I was just a regular twenty-one-year-old going to school and working a job that I'd rather not have been. The girl said goodbye. Philosophy was bringing me down. All I could afford was the same lunch every day. It was routine day in and day out. Beauty is to be found in such circumstances, though.

I wrote this poem in the morning and set out to make this particular day unlike all the others. Sure, I was going to be doing the same things, but now with a different perspective. Sure, I was going to be seeing the same things, but with a different perspective. That perspective was wonder and joy. It's a choice to live such a way despite what so many insist.

I have been no stranger to pain in my life. While it isn't nearly as bad as many have experienced, I have still had my share of happenings that could be considered unfair, and if I were to behave a certain way or make certain decisions, most of American society would probably excuse the behavior on account of how I was raised. I do not buy into this way of thinking, though. Every moment we make the decision on how to respond to situations that come our way. Some of us choose to handle them in a positive manner, looking for the good in the situation or looking for something to be learned from the situation. Still others choose to handle them in a negative manner, seeing only how unfairly they have been treated or seeing only how the world is out to get them. We all know both kinds of people, and I would much rather give my company to the more positive. I would much rather be a person of the more positive type as well.

So as I awoke this particular morning from the previous day of boredom and from another night of only seeing the downside of life and of self-pity and self-loathing, I chose to think and act otherwise. It is very much a choice. There is mystery in the role of the subconscious, but our wills play quite the role as well. I could wake up and loathe, or I could wake up and live the day to its fullest. Not just have the same lunch again, but appreciate it. Not just go to class again, but be full of wonder. And not think too much, but just be. That day was beautiful. That day was full of life and not death. That day was beautiful.

MANLY
MAN

I DON'T want my long hair
Pretty green eyes with
NO I DO NOT ~~HAVE ON MASCARA~~
Eyelashes
Skinny Figure
Undersized T-shirt

~~HIP~~
~~shake~~
~~too~~
~~much~~
when I walk

Confuse anyone...

I AM A MANLY MAN!

Within this sissy frame
obviously rib-laden chest
Lies a heart
that BEATS

to the drum of a
Native American ritual dancing
~~WILDNESS~~
It PUMPS an evercascading supply of unTAMEDness
that a herd of WILD mustangs have yet to grasp.

If DANGER lurks about, I will seek it out.
If adventure abounds, there I will be found.
If a damsel be in distress

I will show her who is best

I AM A MANLY MAN!

Because I DON'T FLUSH
and I leave the lid up.

I drive a nineteen
eighty-eight
Ford PICK-UP truck.

GIRLS DON'T BREAK UP WITH ME
I break up with them FIRST!
(except the last time)

I DON'T SHAVE THE HAIR ON MY FACE
(because I still can't grow facial hair yet...
but when I CAN, I won't)

BECAUSE BEARDS ARE TOUGH!

I
FART
BURP
SPIT
WHEN I WANT

Not caring who is nearby

DISRESPECT my MOMMA
and I will PUNCH you in the eye!

I AM A MANLY MAN!

OR AM I?

I TELL MY guy friends I love them.
Sometimes I even hug them
NO I'm not gay

BUT BECAUSE I LOVE THEM.

When I watched *Bambi*
I cried.
WHEN MY MEMA GETS MAD
I still run and hide.

LIKE DAVID I WANT TO BE A MAN AFTER GOD'S OWN HEART
I'm not there yet but past the start.

And when people talk
I try to listen
A SPIRIT OF COMPASSION
that's my vision.
Surely I am a manly man
I WANT TO BE LOVED
and have love
AND GIVE LOVE
(not just that romantic kind either)

ALTHOUGH I AM LOOKING FOR THAT BEAUTY
NOT HELPLESS
But wants to be rescued.
The damsel in distress
MAN
WOMAN
MYTH
TRUE.

CLIMB THE HIGHEST TOWER FOR HER.

LOVE HER.

SHARE with her.

DELIGHT IN HER.

Be her WARRIOR

HER PROTECTOR

SHE WILL BE MY CROWN
and I will be hers.

~~MY MASCULINITY~~ WILL BE PASSED DOWN
AND AFFIRMED TO MY SONS.

Each of my daughters will know they are LOVELY
and deserving of authentic romance.

SOCIETY TELLS ME
ALL DAY LONG

THAT I HAVE DEFINED MANHOOD
COMPLETELY WRONG

BUT YOU ASK any honest man and he will agree
YOU ASK any honest woman and she too will see

THAT I AM A MANLY MAN!

CONCERNING "MANLY MAN"

I'm five foot eleven, 125 pounds, and a pretty boy by most people's standards, so I am definitely not the manliest in terms of the physical. Just the other day I was looking at some old photographs of me around the junior high years, and I understood why I was picked on so much. It wasn't until my junior year in high school that I got over the ninety-pound mark. And I believe when I started my senior year of high school, I was still only five foot four. I was a late bloomer. Embarrassingly late. Like I'm embarrassed to even write about this. I have leg hair now, though, so I don't have to lie about being on the swim team anymore (I was at one point, but that's not why I didn't have any man hair on my legs). During the eighth grade I got sick of the bowl haircut, so I grew my hair out, and then I looked like a twelve-year-old girl. "Faggot" was to be heard nearly every day. Anywhere I went, I was called Miss or Ma'am. As I walked into the men's room, violent, staring glances and comments like "this is the men's room" were frequently heard. Even today I get this, only it is not because I am genuinely thought to be a girl, but often it wasn't when I was younger either. People are just genuinely mean, and I don't fit into the standard jock look. It's ridiculous. But no matter, I am content with my body and my look and who I am as a person, so harsh comments and stares fall on deaf ears and blind eyes. Or maybe they don't. Maybe my response to the criticism of the way I look or the things I do is "Manly Man."

A friend of mine named Andrew told me about a book called *Wild at Heart* by John Eldredge. It inspired Andrew so much that he decided to move out of his home and primarily camp for two months. Something inside of Andrew came alive as he read *Wild at Heart*, and he set out to discover what that was. For much of his life he lived in fear of one thing or another and always felt held back by something within himself. There was no adventure. No love fought for. No proper way for him to express himself. It was only after Eldredge's book that he found that expression and that release. So he turned me onto the book as well. And I too felt something leap within. Much of the book is about "manly things" like camping or adventure and fighting for that girl, all themes central to a man's life, Eldredge argued. And what it did for me was allow me to be accepting of my manhood. That I am by design set for adventure. That I am by design wanting to fight for a love. That I am by design called to lead.

And so I wrote "Manly Man." It is a challenge to modern-day thought of what manhood actually is because so many don't know. I still struggle with what manhood is. How alike are men and women? Is it really only culture that decides how men and women are to behave? Does a man have to play sports and have nice pecs to be a man? And on and on. I do not like the way many have defined manhood, but I have come to grips with my own manhood.

I've recently started sewing, and as I was sewing, I received a phone call from a friend.

"What are you doing?" he asked.

"Just sewing some pillows," I replied.

"Bradley, you are about one manicure away from being a homosexual."

And then we laughed together. I might not be understood by all, but that is really of no importance. I am comfortable with who I am and my ways. And I will continue to learn to sew.

NO SHE DIDN'T, OH NO SHE DIDN'T WRITE THAT

(ANNIE PART II)

She used words like:

THIS.

and

STUFF.

and

WHATEVER.

and ...

Well, I'm SORRY
But I like to think
of what we HAD
as a little bit more
than these misplaced
words English
you're using
that only SERVE
to make me

SAD

and

CONFUSED

and

BELITTLED.

And make me seem
SO TRIVIAL.

Be CIVIL, girl!

NO SHE DIDN'T ...

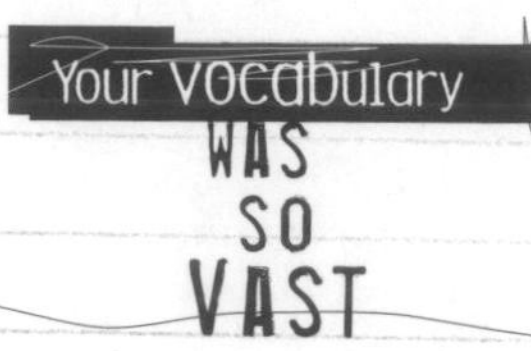

Your vocabulary
WAS
SO
VAST

I even bought a
300,000-word
dictionary
to keep up
with your______

BUT now you break it all down
with ambiguous words like:

THIS.
and
STUFF.
and
WHATEVER.
and...

What in the world were YOU
THINKing, little lady?

YOU'RE ACTING
SO STINKIN' SHADY!
But I'm not going
to THINK about it.
Moving along,

NEXT POEM!

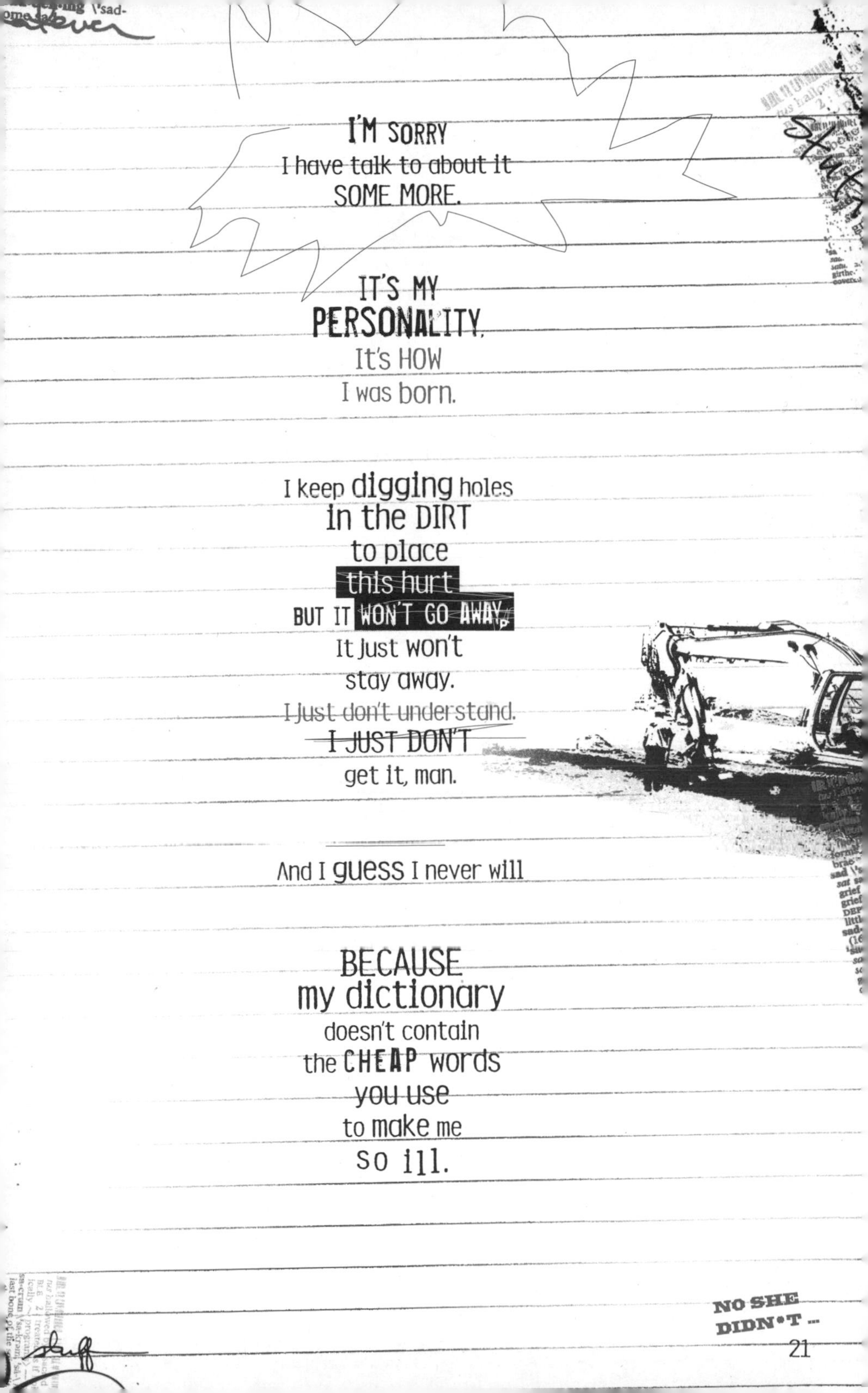

I'M SORRY
I have talk to about it
SOME MORE.

IT'S MY
PERSONALITY.
It's HOW
I was born.

I keep digging holes
in the DIRT
to place
this hurt
BUT IT WON'T GO AWAY.
It just won't
stay away.
I just don't understand.
I JUST DON'T
get it, man.

And I guess I never will

BECAUSE
my dictionary
doesn't contain
the CHEAP words
you use
to make me
so ill.

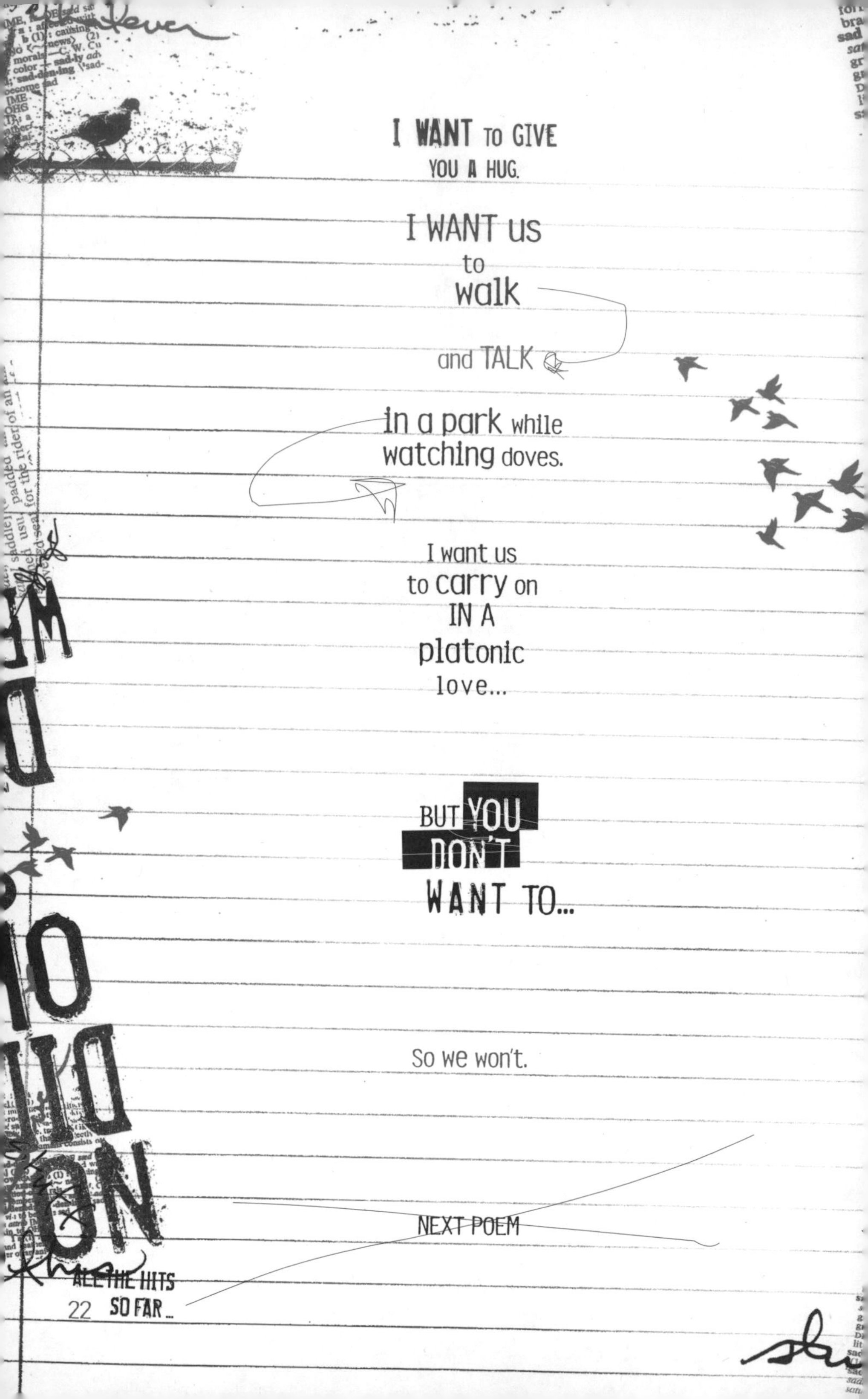
I WANT TO GIVE
YOU A HUG.
I WANT us
to
walk
and TALK
in a park while
watching doves.
I want us
to carry on
IN A
platonic
love...
BUT YOU
DON'T
WANT TO...
So we won't.
NEXT POEM

NO SHE DIDN'T, OH NO SHE DIDN'T

CONCERNING "NO SHE DIDN'T, OH NO SHE DIDN'T WRITE THAT (ANNIE PART II)"

Getting dumped stinks. No way around that fact. It hurts. Sometimes it hurts really badly, and other times it's a relief. But this instance was no relief. This was no happy-she-dumped-me-first-so-now-I-don't-have-to-dump-her. This was pain. This was confusion. This kept me up at night asking questions like "What the ...?" "How come ...?" "I don't get ..." and on and on. I analyzed it. I dissected it. I thought of everything that was ever said with mouth and body. I asked friends. I asked strangers. I asked Brother Sun and Sister Moon. And, of course, I asked her. Maybe more than once I asked her. Maybe more than twice even. I don't know how many times, but she says that it was "all we ever talked about," so I stopped talking and put it in a letter. I read it to my ex-stepmother to see if she thought it was too much or too little or too something that I didn't want to have in there but couldn't personally see because I was so blinded by passion and less guided by reason.

"Wow, Brad," she said. "That's beautiful." Then she praised me some more and said she would like me to write something for her if she ever needed some sort of reconciliation letter.

I mailed that three-plus-page baby the next day with a confidence that what was said was deserving of an appropriate response with the full honesty, sincerity, and integrity that I applied when writing my side of it. What I got was a paragraph of teenage girl gibberish. Oh boy, oh boy, was I ticked! And she used those little words I say she used. And those little punctuation marks that can mean a few different things. I searched for meaning in every hidden space between every single letter. To be honest, I read it so many times that I memorized most of it. Lame-o.

This poem was my response to her letter. This poem was my response to our relationship.

Getting dumped is hard, like I've already said, and most of us already know that. To have someone say they would rather not be in your company any longer and to know that someone doesn't want to talk to you for hours about nothing on the phone any longer sucks. Aside from the couple of girls I went steady with before it counted for anything, this was my first real relationship, and it only lasted a few short months. (How quickly our hearts can be given away to another!) What I found hardest to deal with was the bitterness. Once some of the hurt went away, it showed its ugly head and stuck around for a while.

On the surface, bitterness seems to be a good idea. When we've been wronged by another unfairly, our first reaction is hurt, and bitterness quickly covers the hurt. It's the wrapping paper over the package. It's most certainly a natural thing, too. Bitterness is in our blood, but forgiveness lies in the blood of the One who conquered all evil, which includes bitterness. So when we are hurt, we become bitter, and our once-pure love for the other person has become everything except pure. Where before we would put the other person before ourselves and love them as unselfishly as we knew how, we now place ourselves first, and the one who hurt us not just in the back of the line but out of the line altogether. Out of sight. Out of our consciousness if we could. We no longer wish them good, but disaster. No more wishing them well. Rather, we wish them hell. Sorry about the rhyme there. But we really do wish them hell because they hurt us. And no one is supposed to hurt us. But this bitter paper we have wrapped ourselves in only ends up hurting us.

What once seemed a good idea because it was the most natural and most easy has turned into an ulcer on our hearts, affecting how we forever view others around us. And we carry that bitterness near our conversation, so on occasion others are brought down as we belittle the other with our words and make fools of ourselves with our unseen-to-us shame. So on and on we go. And on and on we carry this chip on our shoulder. And on and on we distance ourselves from our fellow humans and even God. How so? Because we cannot carry bitterness in our hearts and expect to see God.

"We love because he first loved us. If anyone says, 'I love God,' yet hates his brother, he is a liar. For anyone who does not love his brother, whom he has seen, cannot love God, whom he has not seen. And he has given us this command: Whoever loves God must also love his brother." (1 John 4:19-21)

"Therefore, if you are offering your gift at the altar and there remember that your brother has something against you, leave your gift there in front of the altar. First go and be reconciled to your brother; then come and offer your gift." (Matt. 5: 23-24)

Only the Lord can fully restore a heart destroyed by bitterness. It is not up to us to change the other's position or heart. It is not up to us to control the outcome of the situation. We are only to have a right heart in the matter. Sometimes it will not work out as one hopes it should, as was the case for a long time with the girl spoken of in this poem. I was still treated poorly, and reconciliation would not come until a year and a half later. But long before that, I had forgiven her, so her response to me could no longer harm me. And I asked the Lord of Forgiveness to forgive me for the way I behaved prior to letting love lead my actions and for the way I let bitterness take root in my heart. And then I wished her well in life. When one is trapped in bitterness, he cannot wish the one who hurt him good because too much pain and selfishness are blocking his eyes.

We don't have to be friends with everyone, but we do have to love everyone. Bitterness cannot walk alongside love.

ON BEING JOYFUL AND CONTENT

I'M ECSTATIC!

and my Thoughts
are
UNCONTROLLABLY
sporadic!

Yet centered around one center...

JOY.

In PLUSH ripe tones
JOY IS RUSHING THROUGH MY BONES!

If JOY were a color
It would be
PURPLE
pastel
PRETTY

Like Old women and young children
both wear on EASTER

Smiling while having deviled eggs
and drinking KOOL-AID

Chasing
BLOWN
bubbles
in the BACKyard

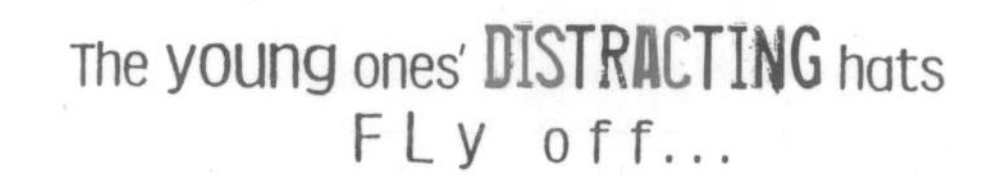

And the old ones laugh
a contagious laughter
That is to be shared
by EVERYONE there.

The sun
SHINES down upon them
as all of their physical impeRfections
GLEAM
beautifully

and Inside.
INSIDE
I feel like THIS
And I look OUTside my window
and imagine the
future PURPLE pastel PRETTY
MOMENTS OF JOY
that I will one day have with my wife.
My children.
My friends.
My family.

I REALLY look forward to those moments
But I am thankful for the one
THAT I am having right now.
This morning.

Alone.
On my couch.

OVERWHELMED by JOY.

CONCERNING "ON BEING JOYFUL AND CONTENT"

I like to think of myself as a relatively simple man. I wear the same pair of pants every day. I eat cheap food and don't care if salt and pepper grace my potatoes or not because I like to accept the taste the food itself has to offer. I don't own too many things. I like to sit under the sky and watch the clouds or admire the contrast of the blue in the sky with the green on the leaves of trees. For many, the thought of being happy to just sit on a couch and look out the window is preposterous. Our world is thriving on busyness and being entertained. But I want nothing of it most of the time. Give me a comfortable couch or the floor. Not so for our culture. It is now, and it is their way or no way. It's unfortunate because with such an overly busy and selfish life, I don't see true joy being possible. And if one is always doing something, how can he ever process what is happening to him? If one is never content, how can he ever know peace? It's very tricky and at only twenty-three, I can say I don't have it figured out. My heart is often restless too. But it is in the simple that I am seeking contentment and deep joy.

Just yesterday I came to think of a new aspect of the joy phenomenon. Now, I make no claim to know hardly anything about joy, for I can only say what I have experienced. And maybe it is only happiness that I speak of in this poem and have incorrectly named it joy. Whatever it is called by whoever decides to define things makes no difference to me. Anyway. As C.S. Lewis spoke of joy in *Surprised by Joy*, I have these moments where I'm emotionally elated. I'm overwhelmed with a good feeling and only know to call it joy. It's almost ridiculous how it expresses itself sometimes. An ever-present smile or fidgety rocking motion or seeing everything good as worthy of praise to God. And I'm carried away with emotion as if on a drug or something. Some say this is no good and should be brought in and contained because it is so fleeting. And it is. It is not this tangible feeling of joy that I seek because as quickly as it comes, it will leave. Still, though, it is nice to feel every now and again. But recently I have come to experience something beyond the pleasurable feeling of joy and have felt its deeper companion: hurt. Have you ever known so much joy that it hurt? And so much joy that you are stunned before God and feel so inadequate to have known such a joy?

I think I now have.

I've been on tour the past week and have experienced the following things worth mentioning:

> Sharing the Christian message in an unwelcoming environment and being yelled at repeatedly to shut up cuss word cuss word.
>
> Hearing a kid share his excitement of how God is using him to bring two friends together.
>
> Seeing the love friends have for one another.
>
> Being involved in a high-speed police chase while not even realizing it and having guns pulled on my traveling buddies and me by furious police officers (all because we thought we didn't pay the highway toll).
>
> Going to the ghetto of west Chicago and attending a church where I was greeted not by handshakes but hugs, experiencing their love, and then eating fried chicken with them.
>
> Meeting six white missionary kids who live on $17 a week and volunteer their lives to ministry in the ghetto of Chicago.

These are simple things to many minds but beautiful and complex to this one. For I have seen God in all of them and have been nothing but humbled by each of them. And I've been on overload with such recent experiences that I have broken down and become "as though dead."

The Christian Bible contains stories of people who have actually encountered God, seen His face or His glory. They did not jump for joy. They were not overcome with the good feeling that joy sometimes brings. They did not smile. They did not call a friend and share what good things they had seen. No. They fell to the ground as though they were dead. They were blinded. They asked the Lord to leave their presence. They repented of their sin. They acknowledged the holiness of God and the distance between Him and themselves. So I have been, too, these past few days. And I'm starting to think it is a deeper sense of joy that I'm experiencing as I continually encounter God throughout my days, be it in the presence of others or alone on my couch meditating upon the goodness of God. There are sure to be more days ahead of the purple pastel pretty kind, but the days of the more aching joy will be present as well.

BIG THINGS IN BIG PACK-AGES

There's this

FAT

FAT

lady on
DA beach.

JIGGLE
Roll
JIGGLe

One-piece-tie-dye-swimsuit

bouncing

ROUND
and
ROUND.

SHE Sets her things down
Waddles up to the water
Gets her shins wet

Looks a r o u n d
and smiles.

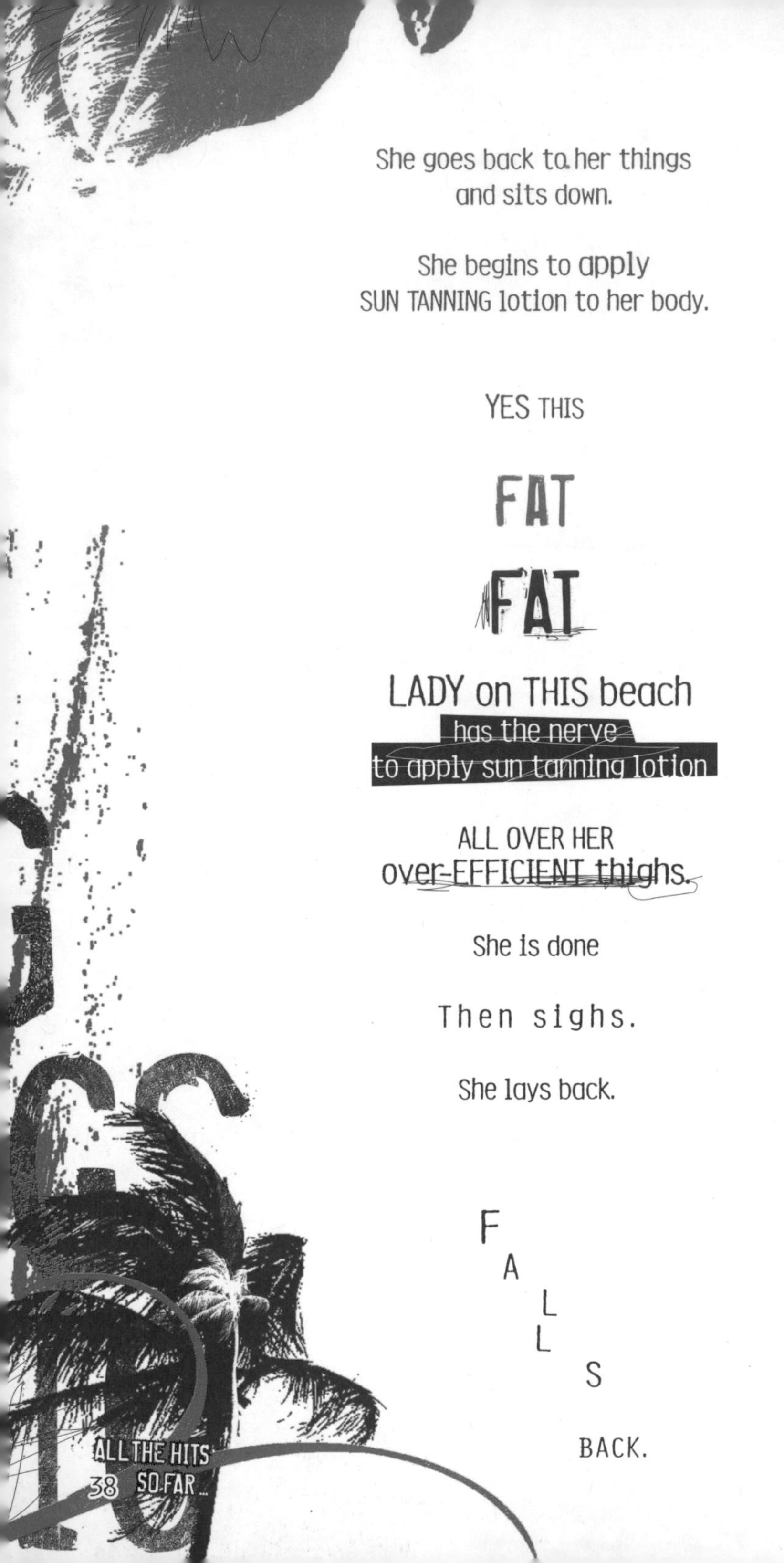

She goes back to her things
and sits down.

She begins to apply
SUN TANNING lotion to her body.

YES THIS

FAT

FAT

LADY on THIS beach
has the nerve
to apply sun tanning lotion

ALL OVER HER
over-EFFICIENT thighs.

She is done

Then sighs.

She lays back.

F
A
L
L
S

BACK.

She closes her eyes
and begins to sunbathe.

SHE IS CONTENT

And don't care.

SHE IS BEAUTIFUL!
Don't anyone dare.

GOD'S FIXED

and His
eyes stare...

"if only they all loved as that beauty there"

CONCERNING "BIG THINGS IN BIG PACKAGES"

It saddens me to routinely discover that so many girls are insecure about their bodies and don't feel pretty. This woman on the beach, whom I saw in Florida, was no such girl, though. She had found such confidence in herself! Such contentment with her body! And it was clear in her dress and behavior.

She was beautiful. With her visor, mesh bag, tie-die skirt, ballerina-like bikini outfit, big smile. She was not routinely adjusting her bathing suit or making sure her hair was in perfect placement or looking over her shoulder. No. She just was who she was and proud to be so. The hot babes walking along did not carry the beauty that this women had all about her. While I'm not denying that some "bodies" are more attractive than others, I do believe that inner beauty most definitely affects outer beauty more than people ever say. Who cares if everybody is not like a supermodel?

No one ever says that, though. A walk through the mall or a flip through the television makes that clear in a matter of moments. Television influences culture, so watch the scandalously dressed girl get the attention from men. See the loose girl drive the youthful boys wild. Half-naked women with the most lustful presence are seen everywhere, and the average girl without the biggest boobs and hottest legs cannot compete and is left to feel sub-par to what media and her culture have told her she should be. This doesn't just hurt girls, either. Men and boys are led to believe that every girl should be like the babes in the magazines. Many males, driven by sight and controlled by hormones, follows after the prettiest and thinnest and wildest and sexiest.

Some guys have believed the lie that the beauty of the female body resides in only one form. That there is no room for diversity. That if every girl does not look like the elite few do, she is not worthy of his affection. The female's self-esteem is then shot. She only compares herself to others and never matches up. She is never comfortable, never secure, never content. Neither is the male because he soon finds that he needs more than just a beautiful body to bring him joy. Hence, broken hearts, broken relationships, broken families.

This cycle has to stop. Let's start loving each other for who we are and not how we look.

> *Your beauty should not come from outward adornment, such as braided hair and the wearing of gold jewelry and fine clothes. Instead, it should be that of your inner self, the unfading beauty of a gentle and quiet spirit, which is of great worth in God's sight. For this is the way the holy women of the past who put their hope in God used to make themselves beautiful. (1 Pet. 3:3-5)*

THE ANNOYING HARDCORE DUDE THAT GOES TOO FAR

I AM
HARDCORE!

I will WINDMILL KICK you in the face
EVERYBODY BACK UP,
make a circle,

THE LIGHTS ARE LOW,
AND I'M ABOUT TO
GO...OFF!

HERE COMES THE BREAKDOWN...
KAR-A-TE CHOP!

RAISE UP YOUR ARMS,
MAKE AN X IF YOU'RE DOWN.
me and my crew

WE OWN
THIS STINKIN' TOWN!

WATCH OUT FOR MY FIST,
Your FACE it will kiss.
ON PURPOSE.

I'm TOUGH and I'm ticked.

I don't slow dance,
I DON'T SALSA DANCE,
forget the tango,

I DON'T
slam
DANCE
you IDIOT!

I DANCE HARDCORE!

On the FLOOR I'm the man you've never seen before.
When the drummer yells
"GO"
...it's my time to blow!

and in between songs I yell at the band,
because I DON'T CARE
what they have to say

I'm not here to learn
anything
ANYWAY.

I'm here to DANCE,
in the ZONE,
in a trance.

I DON'T smoke cigarettes,
but if she's willing,
I'll drop my pants.

PROMISCUOUS I AM,
(but I'm vegan, I don't eat MEAT,
or any of that stuff
cuz it's bad for you, right?)

SAVE THE ANIMALS,
forget the sweatshop scandals

I DO NOT SHOP
AT HOT TOPIC!

I AM NOT MALLCORE!

I AM HARDCORE!!!

MADBALL,
HATEBREED,
THROWDOWN,
and TERROR,

I own all their records on colored vinyl,
LIMITED EDITION
and hand numbered.

But you won't see me askin' for no AUTOGRAPH.

I **AIN'T** LOOKIN LIKE **NO FOOL**.

If they AIN'T Screamin',

I AIN'T listenin'.

If they AIN'T got a
B L A S T BEAT,
I AIN'T tappin' my feet.

I EAT EMO PANSIES FOR BREAKFAST!
and give their little T-shirts to my little sister.

So cry about it
you messenger bag purse carrying...
WHATEVER.

I WEAR GIRL PANTS,
but I'm homophobic.

Yet, the way I'm always huggin'
on my HOMEBOYS
you sure wouldn't know it.

I've had my EARS
stretched an inch
Since back in '96

SOMEBODy told me

HARDcore

was a place to share what you believe

but I DIDN'T like what dude said,
so I FLIPPED him off
and told him to leave.

I'M MAD AT SOCIETY
cuz my parents
won't buy me a new computer,
(even though I asked politely).

My PlayStation 2 is BROKEN

when that breaks though,
SOMETHIN' is gonna HIT THE FAN,
and I'll EXPRESS myself with

Just like a man.
cuz that's how it's done,

right?

YOU get MAD,
and start a FIGHT,

RIGHT?

I THINK I may,

I think I MIGHT,

TAKE my insecurities out
on that PUNK

IN
THE
PIT
TONIGHT!

CUz really I am just insecure.

MORE THAN THAT
I'm kinda scared,
and I'm hurting inside,
and I don't know how to deal with it.

I don't know what being a MAN means.

I THOUGHT ACTIN' TOUGH...
WAS the way to go.

but now that I think about it,

I'M EMO!!!

THE ANNOYING HARDCORE DUDE THAT GOES TOO FAR

CONCERNING "THE ANNOYING HARDCORE DUDE THAT GOES TOO FAR"

Every band has a hit. Or at least every band wants to have a hit. I'm not a band, but this poem is my hit for sure. While it's not getting spins on the radio and I still don't have any money, it's the one most requested at shows. I like that for a couple reasons. First, to have people yelling out to do such and such poems is just funny. Because it's a poem, ya know. Who yells out poem requests? Second, it's one of the more recently written from this collection, so that makes me think my newer stuff doesn't suck all that bad since it's one that kids really want to hear.

For the person who doesn't go to hardcore shows or know anything about hardcore, he won't understand many of the things going on within this poem. And to be honest, it would be too huge of an endeavor to explain all of the little details that make this poem what it is. So if you are the person who doesn't know anything about hardcore, sorry to say I'm not going to explain it here. Instead, I'll briefly point out a few of the main themes and then carry on.

One is finding a balance and being consistent in one's belief system. For example, many within the scene are heavily into animal rights and promoting and discussing the proper treatment and rights of animals. Vegetarianism is cool. Veganism is even cooler. Very rarely, though, do I ever hear discussion of human rights pertaining to sweatshops or slave trading or child prostitution or any other humanitarian issue from the AIDS crisis in Africa to poverty in America. Something is awfully wrong with this, and I wanted to point this out.

The other main theme of the poem is that of manhood. Unfortunately, many males are still convinced that being a man is defined by acting tough all the time, but most of us know what such men are like on the inside.

No, I'm not promiscuous, and no, I'm not homophobic. Of all the poems contained herein, this and "The Celebration Wedding" are the only ones that are not directly speaking about myself. While I do identify with many of the things written in this poem, I am not the primary character within it. Too often I get people confusing me for the character of the poem, and then they get mad at me and say things out of ignorance that they should not say.

And for the record, I have loved hardcore music for the last nine years. I am not anti-hardcore or anti-dancing. I am all for it. However, I, along with most people who love the hardcore scene, am upset with some of the things that go on and are allowed to go on within the scene. "The Annoying Hardcore Dude That Goes Too Far" is my way of communicating some of those concerns in a lighthearted manner.

I FELT REALLY GOOD THIS DAY, YES

You're pouring your love ALL OVER ME!
It's dripping off the

TOPS

And sides

And bottoms

And middles

Of trees full of ~~splendid little~~ busy bees

about doing their purpose

HOW
CAN THIS BE?

That you've let my HEART to see?
And experience?
And take in?

AND NOW
to sing.

SING! Sing! SING!

About your love to everybody. ANYBODY.
Or the somebody that's considered a nobody

But THEY are special to thee.

I FELT REALLY ...

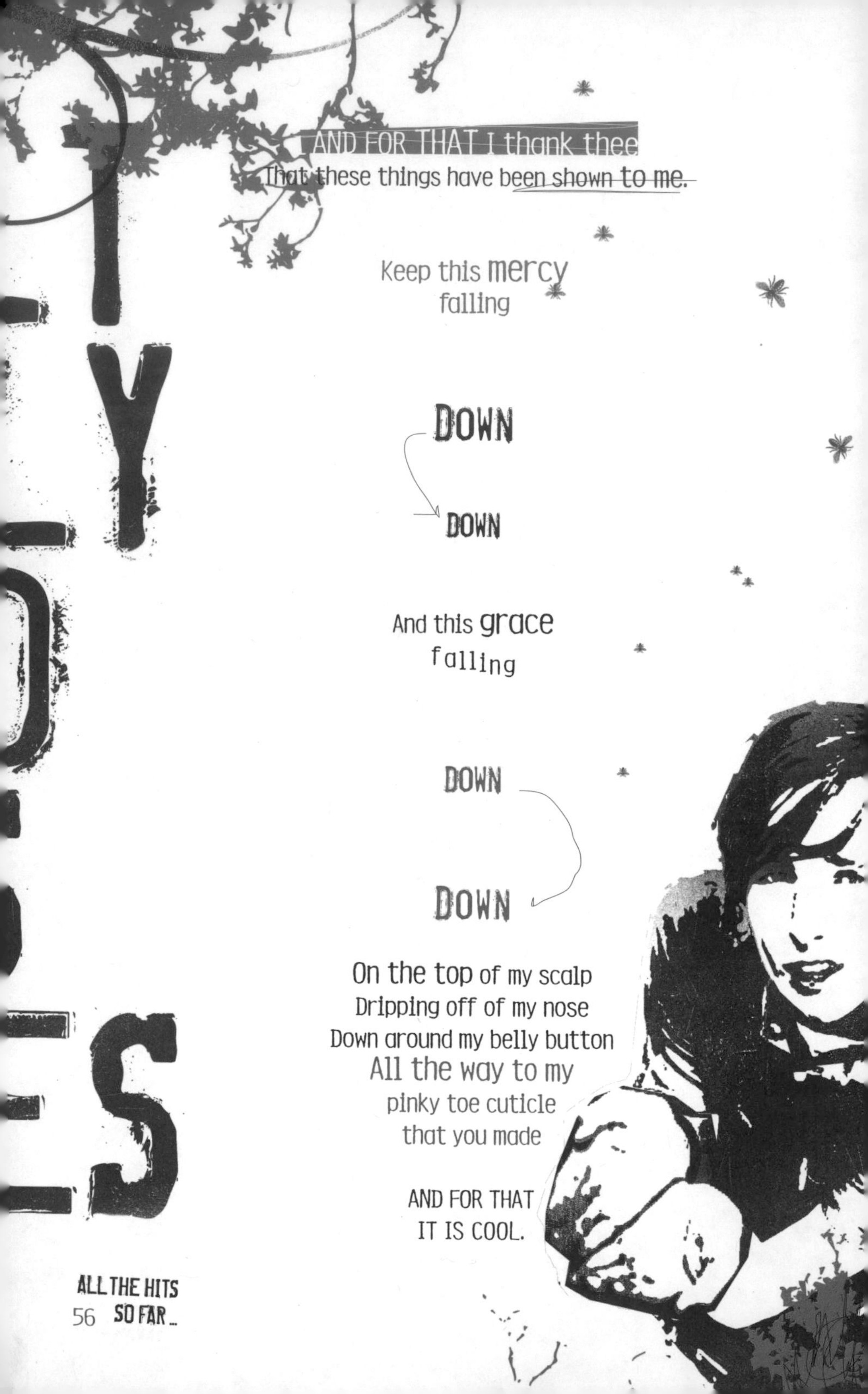

AND FOR THAT I thank thee
That these things have been shown to me.

Keep this mercy
falling

DOWN

DOWN

And this grace
falling

DOWN

DOWN

On the top of my scalp
Dripping off of my nose
Down around my belly button
All the way to my
pinky toe cuticle
that you made

AND FOR THAT
IT IS COOL.

SOMETIMES I PLAY THE FOOL
but still your LOVE is all around!

Sprouting from the ground

HERE

and There

Everywhere!

ESPECIALLY ON THIS FLOOR that I now stand.
How amazingly awesome is your plan
That cannot be thwarted by any man

No matter how big

OR STRONG

Or UGLY

Or EVIL he BE.

Because through you is victory.
And it's victory that I now SPEAK of
and have to LET OUT of my skin

Because for too long it has been contained therein.

Lord, I praise you because you're DIFFERENT.

AND efficient.

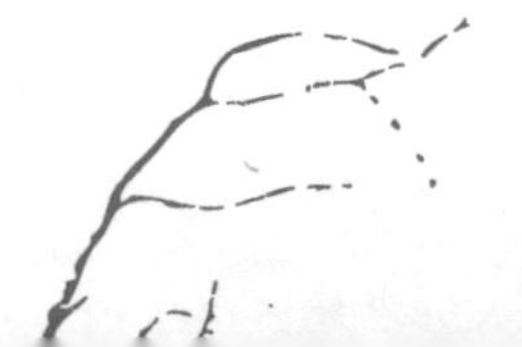

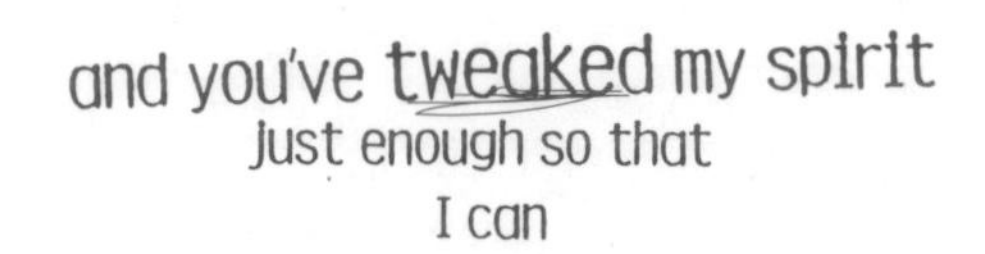

just enough so that

I can

TASTE

and

SEE

that YOU truly are good

PINEAPPLE

for the first time

in my mouth.

OR THE WARMTH OF YOUR SUN

on the BACK

of my

NOT
WARM
NECK

on a

NOT
WARM
DAY.

I'LL PRAISE YOUR NAME TODAY.

and Tomorrow.

FOREVER.

FELT REALLY GOOD THIS DAY, YES

CONCERNING "I FELT REALLY GOOD THIS DAY, YES"

Two months prior to the writing of this poem I had the privilege of hearing and seeing poet Clayton Scott perform. He was a former pastor of mine for a brief time, and I'd been hearing that he began performing poetry and was even starting to make a living at it, so I was glad to see him. I was not expecting to be so impressed. I was blown away, in fact. My previous experience with slam poetry was just some mad dude dropping f-bombs all over the place and being ticked at white people. Clayton talked about pizza or dancing or God having "hair like Don King, playing guitar like B.B. King, and having Tourette's just to throw a twist into the mix." He talked about simple things but made them out to be so much bigger, and I thought this was an amazing way to communicate. I even joked with a friend about me writing poetry.

"You should," he said. "You'd be good at it."

But I never thought of actually doing it. The thought was there for the moment, and then I went on about my life as usual. Until about two months later, on January 19, 2003, when I was forced to begin writing.

I say "forced" because it came on me with such a force. Not a gentle whisper or a soft breeze, have a cup of lemonade, chill out on the grass, did you feel that brush against my arm force. The first few lines came to me, and I just knew I had to write it down. So I pulled over along a beautiful spot off Highway 71 south in northwest Arkansas and scrambled to find a scrap of paper and pen to start writing. And I wrote. What came out was "I Felt Really Good This Day, Yes" in its near entirety. In fact, I don't know if anything about it has changed since then. Immediately, I called up my good friend Spence and read it to him, and we both just laughed about it.

"Dude! I wrote a poem, man! Listen!" I laughed.

And he did. And then he laughed and said it was pretty cool. We hung up, and I sat in my truck and kept reading it aloud to myself. It was fun. It felt good. I loved the way it sounded, and I enjoyed the rhyme and the flow and the feel of saying "... trees full of splendid little busy bees ..." and then I went home and wrote some more. And they just kept coming. And now here I am a published poet, ha-ha.

Sometimes I get these fits of overwhelming joy and excitement. It's a flood of emotion where the simple just becomes so beautiful and the mundane so complex and full of mystery. Around this time I remember starting to fall in love with nature. I was taking a zoology class at that time and had previously taken biology, but the specifics of biology I didn't get, and to this day I can't say that I really learned anything specific in there. At least I can't remember the metamorphosis of a flower or nitrogen's role in the cosmos or anything like that. Nope. I learned it for the test, but what I learned more was just wonder. I found it hard to ever get past just looking at the flowers instead of learning their parts. And a water puddle after a rain would become an endless source of wonder and entertainment. Have you seen the things that swim around in a puddle after a good day's rain? I never had before. Or those little orange-and-black bug worm cocoon things that show up at spring and stick to doorposts or other random places? Those turn into ladybugs.

These little things only led to my wonder of God and how cool He was for making all this stuff. And this wonder and this joy began to express itself outside of myself through poetry. I did nothing voluntarily. It just happened to me. Plato said something of the sort ... that poets really don't know anything, something just hits them, and they are inspired to write. So goes it with me. Because I didn't choose to write. It chose me, if you will.

A little bit on pineapples ... I remember the day I first had a piece of fresh pineapple. I don't remember if I randomly decided to buy it or if someone suggested one to me or what, but regardless, I had a fresh pineapple on my kitchen cabinet. And the first bite blew me away. It sounds silly, doesn't it? To be so taken with a piece of fruit? But I never knew what pineapple was supposed to taste like! Canned was the only way I had known. So I remember being stoked after eating my first chunk. And it is this joy in these simple, silly things that I hope to maintain throughout my life. How cool it would be to have such a pleasure and joy in such simple things as fruit, bugs, and God's love.

SHORT AND UN-TITLED

They say that

"sometimes
you're further
than the
MOON

and

SOMETIMES
you're closer
than my
skin"

INDEED

I remember back
when you were closer
than MY skin.

THOSE were
the evenings
spent
alone
with you
in bliss.

THOSE WERE
THE MORNINGS
when you
awoke
ME
BY a
gentle
kiss.

And THESE
are evenings
I sit
alone
and WISH
and reminisce

THESE ARE THE MORNINGS
WHEN I AWAKE
to an ALARM clock
After falling asleep

with the hurting
thought

"WHY have YOU forsaken ME?"

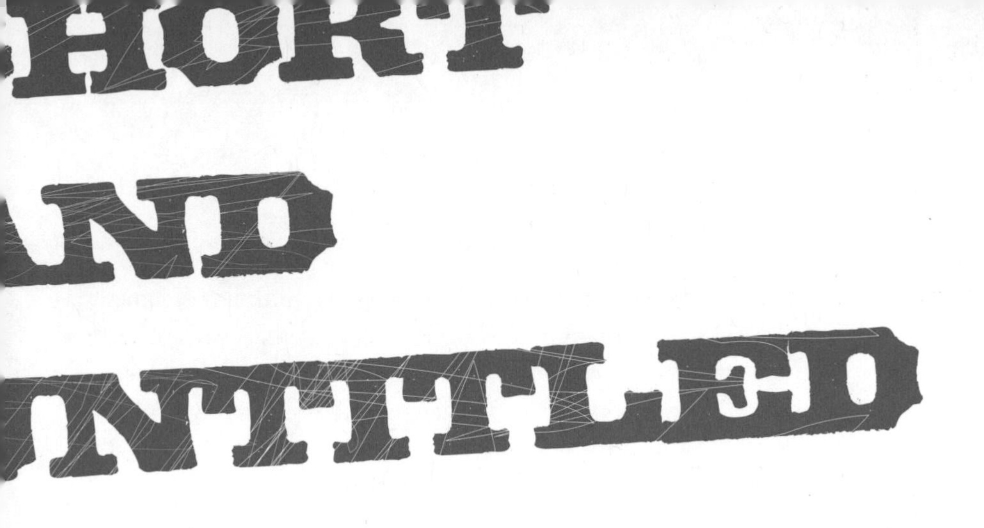

CONCERNING "SHORT AND UNTITLED"

A friend emailed me these lyrics: *sometimes You're further than the moon/sometimes You're closer than my skin.* They're from a song by David Crowder, and while I've never heard it to this day, the words have stuck with me ever since I read them. It's very insightful, and most people who have made a decision to seek after God can relate. Although I don't know that I think it's necessarily right in the literal sense. Does God really leave us? Or is it just our own selves and decisions and psyches messing with us? I am not versed enough in the scriptures to thoroughly answer that, but I lean toward the thought that God never forsakes us. More often than not, it seems to just be my own self getting confused and relying too much upon feeling rather than truth.

So goes this poem. No, I do not think I was actually abandoned by God, but it seemed that way at the time because the feel-good feelings of being close to God were no longer there. I was hurting. I was alone. I was afraid. I was insecure.

The writer of the Psalms asked God why He had forsaken him, and Jesus Himself asked God that question as He hung on the cross. If those two can ask God the question, then I feel at liberty to ask God where He has gone off to. When it's all said and done, however, I usually find that He was there all along.

THE HUG POEM

I read about how you
touched them

And they were healed

OR EVEN if someone
just touched your CLOAK

THEY WERE FOREVER CHANGED.

You let a broKeN woman
bathe your feet
in her tears

And you washed your best friends' feet.

I'm just wondering, though,

DID YOU ever just
HUG people?

I know it's a silly question and all
I'm sure you would have
(why wouldn't you have?)

BUT it's one of those things
that was NEVER mentioned
And it got me thinking about it

AND HOW
whenever there was a touch
from you
Sins were forgiven
and sickness fell

~~I think I'm caught up with my sins~~
And LAST TIME I checked
all my body parts are working
NOTHING special HERE

I'm just a kid
with a **HEAVY** HEART
these passing sunrises
and sunsets

I don't think our encounter
would have ended up in your GOSPELS
or anything

BECAUSE ALL I REALLY NEED is a hug
THAT'S OKAY FOR ME TO IMAGINE, RIGHT?
That's not CONFLICTING
with any sort of THEOLOGY, is it?

Okay good.

THEN HUG ME.

BUT NOT one of these
SIDEWAYS one-arm-around-
the-neck type hugs

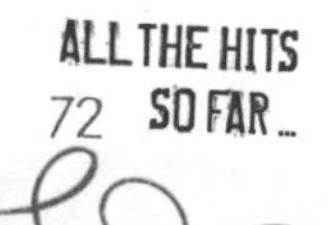

OR the
GHETTO right hand CLASP FISTS
ELBOWS TO CHEST

PAT

PAT

ON THE

BACK

BACK

OR THE you put your RIGHT arm over my LEFT arm
and I put my RIGHT arm under your LEFT arm
And we make this weird SORT-of-
diagonal thing

NAW... none of those!

Take your
old-
SCHOOL
CARPENTER arms
AND THROW THEM AROUND
MY UPPER BODY
leaving my
arms
dangling
underneath yours somewhere
and I can barely move them

BECAUSE you're SQUEEZING me
so HARD.

(But don't pick me up and make my back pop
because I HATE it when people do that.)

And then hold me.

HOLD ME HERE IN YOUR ARMS
until I start to CRY!

BECAUSE
I WANT TO CRY!

but I just can't seem to do it on my own.

I've been teary eyed
ONCE recently
but not even enough
for a

DRIP

Down
my
CHEEK

There's just HURT
in my SOUL
That needs to be purged
SO HOLD ME HERE
in this hugging pose
Until the PAIN
is FLOWING
from my eyes
and nose

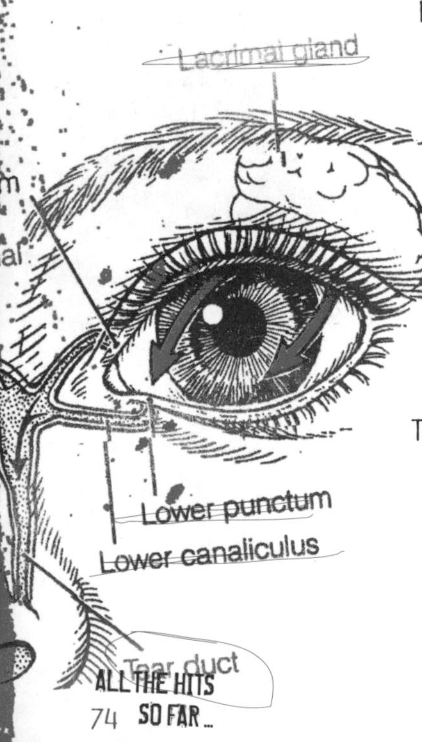

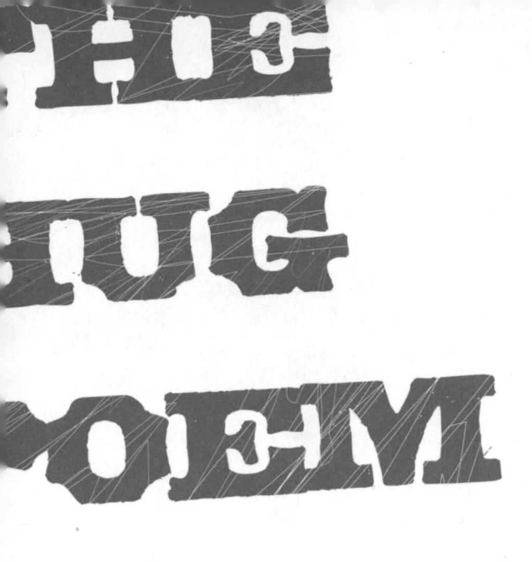

CONCERNING "THE HUG POEM"

Seems like everyone gets to that point in life when they ask, "God, if You are there, show Yourself to me," and perhaps follow up with a few suggested ways in which He can show Himself. In the healing of a loved one. In a perfectly timed falling star. In a miraculous rescue. Should God not do what is requested, the petitioner is left doubting and possibly becoming an atheist. I do not understand the thinking of an atheist.

I have always believed in the existence of God. While I wasn't raised to be an atheist, the religion of my immediate household was not in line with the teachings of Christianity, whether they would agree or not. But the belief of God has always been inside me. Though I sometimes doubt the truths of the Christian faith, a genuine belief in God has never been so shaken that I seriously doubted His existence. Or the existence of an ultimate higher authority (whatever language one wishes to use). Yet, I have come to those points of asking God to reveal Himself further to me. Not His existence, necessarily, but His involvement with myself and humanity. As a Christian, I believe Jesus to be God incarnate. This is not a book of theology, however, so I will leave that statement as is and allow its defense to the writings of the theologians. So, in my believing Jesus to be God, I am asking God to show Himself to me in "The Hug Poem." Not in raising someone from the dead. Not in changing water to wine. Not in giving sight to the blind, but in a simple hug.

I was lonely. I was hurting. And I knew that the only one who could comfort me, who could restore me, who could heal me, who could love on me in the purest and most ultimate sense was the one who promised such things ... Jesus Himself. Yes, the love of God flows through others. In comfort or direction from a fellow believer, God is indeed extending His love to me. But that can only go so far. And as I woke up from another night of unforgiving sleep while staying at a friend's house, I picked up pen and paper and wrote "The Hug Poem."

I needed that closeness. That touch from the divine. That tangible reality that isn't otherworldly or omnipresent or unseen. No, I wanted it to be right in front of me. Seen. Felt. How blessed were those in the time of Jesus! To be a disciple and be with Him always. To share meals with Him. To speak with Him. To walk with Him. To just be with Him. There. Present. Not just in "my heart," as popular Christian jargon says.

One of my favorite scriptures about Jesus involves the woman who touched His garment and was healed. Just by touching His clothing she was healed! How rad is that? Just think what an actual embrace from Him would do. He touched people. And I wonder how He did. Like when He gave the blind man sight ... did He sort of massage his eyes or just spit and make mud, then slap some on the dude's face and go about His business? Or when He healed the leper ... did He just touch him with the tip of His finger or maybe gently rub him? Just the slightest touch from Him would be awesome. But wouldn't there be much more to be had with an actual embrace? The woman who was healed just by touching His clothing, her body was healed, yes. What she set out for was done, yes. But maybe there was even more to be gained if He had hugged her. And as He went about healing people, their bodies were changed forever, and some of them put their faith in Jesus and had love for Him. But if He were to actually hug them, I can't help but imagine they would have been moved even more. They would have been healed emotionally as well as physically. And felt close to Him. It seems He had the power without even needing to touch them because so many were fond of Him, and so many flocked to Him because there was obviously something special about Him. So I cannot even imagine what a hug would have been like.

There is power in touch. Anyone who has ever been

touched even the slightest bit by one whom they love in that more-than-friends way knows this. A bump of the leg. Uh oh! Holding hands? Uh oh! A hug? I have known new lovers to nearly throw up at the first hug from their sweetheart. And it's not just in the realm of romantic love that I speak. Tears flow freely from a well-timed hug to a hurting soul. Or tears of joy at the reunion of long unseen friends. Or the proud hug of a mentor to his pupil on graduation. Or a last embrace to a dying friend. It is in the touch that the rawest of emotions reach their peak. And it is in a hug that two non-lovers can get as near to each other as can be had.

And I wanted that closeness from Jesus Himself.

NEARLY EVERYTHING I'M ABOUT TO SAY... HAS BEEN SAID BEFORE

TALK TO ME
and tell me
that it's
going to be all right

I'm in an awful fright
LONG has been
the night

I'm a lost chick
and I need a hen

Be my hen now, won't you?

Take me under
your feathers
And shield me
from this awful weather

I'm a cliché ship
tossed at sea

~~Wake up~~

~~WAKE UP~~
and rescue me!

Part
this
Red Sea

Tell me to rise
Put dirt
and spit
in my eyes

I believe!

I BELIEVE!

I believe!

I conceive!

I receive!

That you ARE
who you are

You're the
bright morning star
SENT from afar
to bring meaning
to these scars

To bring life
to death
To BREATHE into me
your breath

To GUIDE my path
I'm FINISHING this race
(even if I FINISH last)

but
How long
will this last?
HOW long
~~will this last?~~

The net has been cast
and you have caught me.

May I sip
from your well?

Can YOU
~~sense~~
my
heart
swell?

Have ~~YOU~~ a story to tell?

(I will listen.)

NEARLY EVERYTHING I'M ABOUT TO SAY...

CONCERNING "NEARLY EVERYTHING I'M ABOUT TO SAY ... HAS BEEN SAID BEFORE"

It was months before I realized that there is basically no original thought in this poem. Not to say that anything I've said is original, for there is "nothing new under the sun," but nearly every single line is from a brief mentioning of a happening within the Bible. Particularly revolving around the person of Jesus Christ. Maybe some could say this is lame, and I'm just ripping off the Bible or something, and they may even be right, but when I realized that this was just scripture reference after scripture reference, I sorta got excited. As a Christian, I hope to have the words of the Bible within me to meditate on and allow to guide me. Often I don't feel as if I read and study enough (I don't), but this poem, if nothing else, is like a little gold star next to my name as if I've turned in my elementary school homework. I was encouraged to know that scripture is indeed inside of me and is part of me and on random occasions comes out of me.

Having said that, I have nothing else to add or say.

THERE IS HOPE

There's a heart of such
DISTRESS
that I carry in this CHEST
Please

Reach out and caress
in YOUR pillowesque manner.

Front!

and center!

RIGHT HERE!

and right NOW!

I'm throwing in the TOWEL
I've committed too many fouls

I'VE FLOWN SOUTH

My spirit is turning soUR
I can't go through
ANOTHER hour

BE my precious
pretty
PINK
petite FLower

That blooms
in the night
And LEAD me in the dark
by your MOONlight

I never FOUGHT anywhere
so I thought
And now here I am on these knees
DISTRAUGHT
Crying out to you

PRETTY please!

Pretty PLEASE!

Take this disease
Turning these INSIDES brown
My SMILE turns to FROWN
and my BREATH
smells like DEATH!

BECAUSE I am dead to LIFE
And alive to something
that I don't know you would
have me feel

But this is for REAL

And I need YOU right NOW.

SO SEAL THE DEAL
with your stamp of reGENERATION
And grow me up
into a new creation

TAKEN from a tree
and PLUCKED from a vine

If it's my time to shine
Then shine your light on ME

SO THAT everyone hurting can see

that there is hope.

In a seemingly endless valley
full of ROTTEN fRuit

LEFT BEHIND
from
previous
troops

Who are NOW in YOUR mountains
Drinking directly
from YOUR fountains

SAVE ME a spot.

I will be there
sooner
than
NOT

I'm picking up
the pace
and
slowly

starting

to trot.

THERE IS HOPE

CONCERNING "THERE IS HOPE"

If hope were not so, I would not choose to live.

ANOTHER ONE OF THOSE NIGHTS

SO **WEARY!**
and leery!
and DREARY!

I feel.

~~**STOP**~~ this ~~**MIND**~~
from racing all the time

Restful peace
~~come hither,~~
be **mine.**

It was here
~~earlier~~
but now
it's
LONG
gone
and out of
sight

~~On this~~
~~**RESTLESS**~~
~~**SLEEPLESS**~~
~~**CLOGGED**-up~~
~~left nostril~~
NIGHT.

~~I remember~~

sleep

and WHAT a
comfort
it once
was

BUT NOW
all it does
is leave me
LACKING

Because even there
these thoughts
just
won't
stop
YACKING.

so I

I HIT
the FLOOR
and on
bruised knees
start
BANGING
DOWN
your
DOOR.

~~CAN'T~~
take
this
ANYmore.

HOLY
SPIRIT
MANIFEST
your
BEING

COMFORT this SOUL
SO THAT I CAN
start singing
Of that
peaceFUL
feeling
that any minute now
you'll be bringing.

Grace grows in winter
I am told

(But that's not what I want to hear right now,
truth be known.)

IT'S YOU, FATHER

THAT I DESIRE
SO PUT OUT
this

UNHOLY
FIRE

AND SET ABLAZE
me ANEW
with a peace
that comes
ONLY from you.

WHERE else can I turn
and WHAT
else may I do?

Here I am

Yours.

Here I am

Yours.

Here I am...

Yours.

ANOTHER ONE OF THOSE NIGHTS

CONCERNING "ANOTHER ONE OF THOSE NIGHTS"

I could not tell you the last time I awoke "refreshed" from sleeping. Since I've started traveling the past year, sleep does not come restfully. I never sleep in the same place. I never go to sleep at the same time. I'm in and out of different time zones. A couch to sleep on is rare, even more so a bed. What treasure a bed is! But even restless sleep and an aching back upon awaking are not as crappy as not being able to sleep because of a stopped-up nose. How annoying! Enough about runny noses, though.

I awoke in the middle of the night with this poem in my head. I remember waking up and writing this down and then going back to sleep again. It was just that quick, too. Of all my writings contained herein, this one seems to be the most desperate. It really is, though. I was sick of feeling so crappy. I was sick of the inner turmoil and lack of peace. I was sick of the lack of rest. I was very tired of the greater concept of peace and joy and wanted them to be reduced back to mere emotion: *peaceful feeling that any minute now You'll be bringing.*

I knew what I was going through was just a phase and that the deep, dry well that was myself was soon going to burst with a new, fresh spring. Then happiness would return. Then peace would return. It always does, doesn't it? But I was sick of waiting. Yeah, I knew that grace was growing, and the roots that had grown deep in my times of overflowing were being tested for their strength and endurance. But I didn't want any of that. I just wanted all my trials to be over.

Perhaps the greatest example we have of one's willingness to serve God despite the crud around the situation is the life of Abraham. Abraham did not wish to sacrifice his son Isaac, but he was willing.

I was still *willing* for the Lord to have His way, but I was not completely *allowing* God to have His way with me. I've always had trouble admitting this because I am sinful. I want God's plan for me to somehow be in line with what my plan is. But I still pray for the Lord's will to be done. I still say, "Your kingdom come, Your will be done" and not mine because I know that His ways are higher than my ways. It's important to still pray that prayer of willingness. Even after being so burned out, used up, and tired, I still go to the Lord for restoration because there is no restoration to be had from myself or those around me. There is no peace outside of God. There is no rest, no joy. So I continue to fall to my knees in frustration and desperation, not just asking God for His touch, but demanding it. I am His.

THE CELE- BRATION WEDDING

This is for the ones whose HOPE
is falling

And you no longer hear
your Savior's calling.

This is for the ones whose BACKS
are turning
and that Passion-FILLed HEART you once had
has stopped burning.

This is for the ones
ABANDONED
Now all alone with no solace
and you think that you're STRANDED.

This is for you EMPTY, by life branded
that Had a vision that took leap
but it never landed.

THIS IS FOR the ones who are PLAGUED
by those mysteries of life
And you feel To r n inside
by this mind and spirit strife.

This is for the ones whose desire to do good
IS ALWAYS OUTWEIGHED
and you don't do as you should

This is for the ones whose misstakes mistakes
are too many to count
And the GUILT on your chest
Just continues to mount.

This is for the ones who've been done wrong by SINS
At the coRRuPTeD hands
of perverted men.

HOLD ON.

HOLD ON.

BECAUSE SOON WILL COME THAT CELEBRATION WEDDING
AND BUNDLES OF RESTORATION
WILL BE OUR BEDDING.

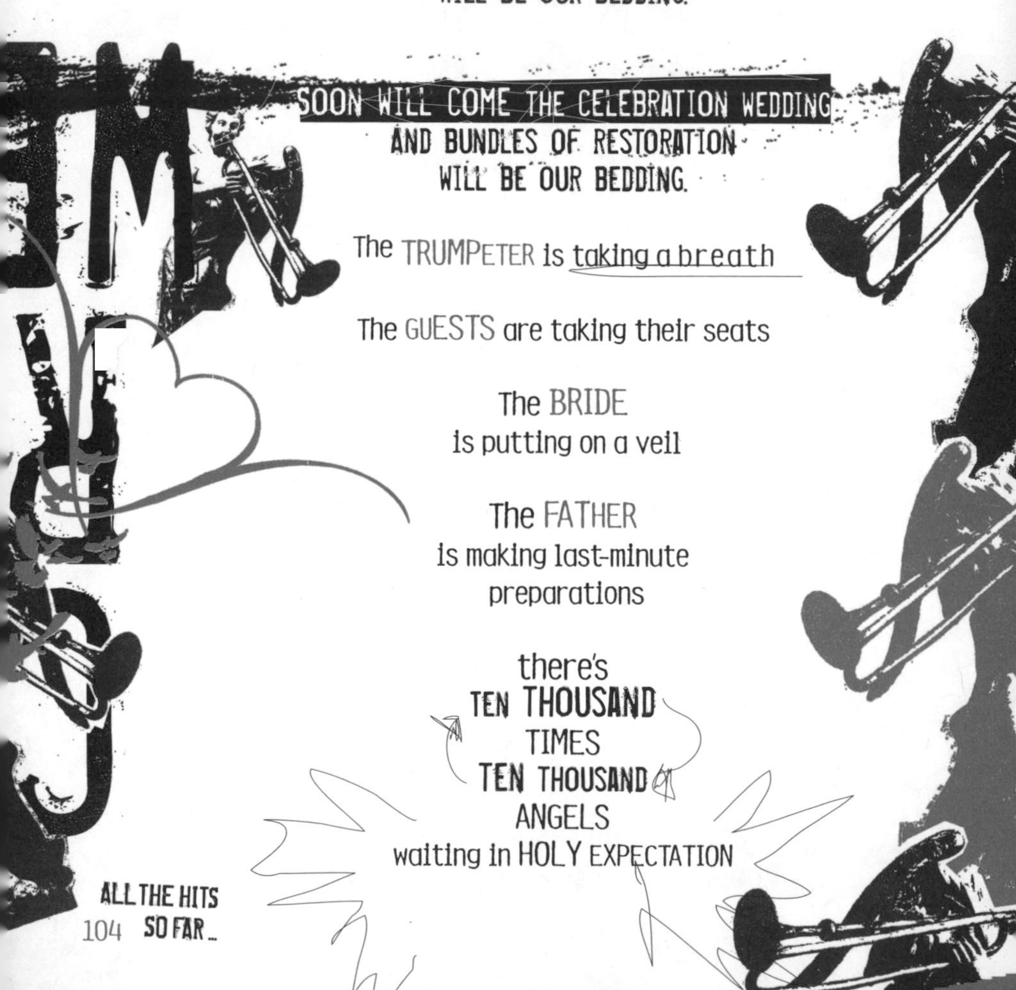

SOON WILL COME THE CELEBRATION WEDDING
AND BUNDLES OF RESTORATION
WILL BE OUR BEDDING.

The TRUMPETER is taking a breath

The GUESTS are taking their seats

The BRIDE
is putting on a veil

The FATHER
is making last-minute
preparations

there's
TEN THOUSAND
TIMES
TEN THOUSAND
ANGELS
waiting in HOLY EXPECTATION

The READIED GROOM IS READY

SOON WILL COME THE CELEBRATION WEDDING

IF YOU ARE
HURTING,
your hurt
will cease.

If YOU are
REstLESS,
you will
FIND peace.

If you are
Empty,
you will
be FILLED.

All of these DOUBTS
and questions
they'll be stilled.

If LIFE for you
is just too trying
Your tears WILL dissipate.
There WON'T be any more crying.

IF THE ONLY THING YOU KNOW
IS SHAME
YOU WILL be cleansed
and never again feel the same

~~IF YOU CAN'T~~

see straight

FOCUS,

persevere,

and WAIT...

SOON WILL COME

THAT CELEBRATION WEDDING

And bundles of
COMPLETE RESTORATION
will be
our bedding.

THE CELEBRATION WEDDING

CONCERNING "THE CELEBRATION WEDDING"

One of my favorite analogies of scripture is the uniting of Jesus and His Church being likened to a wedding. He, the bridegroom, and we, the bride. It implies such an intimacy and commitment. Now some charismatic circles almost take this union literally, and some of their lingo in talking about Jesus makes me a bit uncomfortable. Like I don't want to be romanced by Jesus, ya know? I don't want to have Him kissing me all over. Maybe I just have a misunderstanding of masculinity and affection or something, but where I'm at now, I'd rather have a nice hug minus the lovey-dovey stuff. But I appreciate the

Bible's use of the marriage analogy and find it fitting and beautiful.

More than anything, "The Celebration Wedding" is me banking on a promise. It's the looking forward to that day of being united with my Savior. Oh, how I look forward to it! I am ready to have every tear wiped from my eye. I am ready to have no more worry. I am ready to be absolutely filled with joy. Heaven is my ultimate hope.

and
STATE
Church
CITY
First Holy Communion
STATE
CITY
First Holy Communion Register of this Church
Pastor
Dated
SILENCE

WHAT'S HAPPENING
HERE?

I was once
so ALIVE
and

Now

I'm so full of dread
And almost dead

Show me your wounded hEad
That has led
To communion
with the Father

His presence seems
FARTHER
and
FARTHER
away
each
DAY

But I'm trying so HARD
to steer HIS way
Yet still lonely
and confused
on this
COLD
HARD
GROUND
I LAY

Speak to me with wise mouth and say

"It's all good, kid
it's nothing that YOU did
and though it feels like
I'm not here with you right NOW
Just be still
and listen
for that
sound ..."

(Did you hear it?)

Listen again.

Did you hear it?

That silent voice that just spoke nothing?

THAT IS ME!

I'm LISTENING to your plea
with open ears
COUNTING ALL YOUR TEARS
Flowing from your
irritated eyes
SEARCHING the skies
LOOKING FOR THAT

HOPE

that beyond there lies.
YOU young worrisome sparrow,

FIND REST.

Lay your TATTERED
HEAD upon my
omnipresent breast
And make IT
your nest.

**NO STRONG
COLD
WIND**

COULD EVER BLOW
AND CARRY YOU
from this
your home.

LOOK AROUND
See the LIFE
SPRINGING up from the ground?
Spring colors springing forth
in celebration
of your trusting.

It's a constant PROCESS
this is

Growing you into the person
you are to become

And when you sense the setting of the sun
Know that it's only rising and has just begun.

NOW GO FORTH!

Sing songs
of faith!

Lift up others in the midst of this race
And if you CAN'T keep the pace
or lose sight of my face

Know that I'm always near so you NEED NOT FEAR.
(But don't worry all of them or that right now.)

Just sit here
and enjoy the peace I offer
in my silence.

When I am silent
I am listening.

and Not abandoning.

CONCERNING "SILENCE"

For as little as we actually hear God, I find it interesting that we devote so much of our thoughts and prayers and dialogue expecting to hear Him. I have never heard God's voice audibly, so I can't tell you if His voice is like James Earl Jones or Charlotte Church, but I have experienced that inner voice that demands one's full attention. It's usually followed by a physical reaction or two, such as a fast-pace heartbeat or sweaty palms or fidgety movement. Of course, there is no way of knowing with 100 percent certainty that it actually is God Almighty speaking to you, and many philosophers and anti-Christians will call you a fool for even thinking such a thing. They will press the hearer with questions and blah blah, and the one thinking he just heard God is almost forced to reduce it to his own inner conscious blah blah. Deep down, though, where no one else can tread, we sometimes know it to be God. There is no way of proving it. There is no way of convincing another of its validity. One just knows.

There have been a few times in my life that I was sure of such a happening. When I was in the tenth grade on a school function to Washington, D.C., I went to a McDonald's. Working there was a six-foot-plus, gangsta-looking dude who could have beat me down with little effort. "Tell him that Jesus loves him," I heard in my head and thought it immediately to be God. "Heck, no!" I replied. Scared and unwilling, I walked out and went down the street to eat elsewhere. One of the more recent times was my first show on my first tour. The crowd was punk-rock kids getting wasted. The girls had more pit hair than I did. Plus, punk rockers don't usually want to hear anything about God, or from the Christian religion anyway, so there I was, about to tell them through poetry, and I was very much intimidated. I prayed to God telling Him that I couldn't and didn't want to do it and how scared I was. He said "If you don't tell them of My love, then who will?" This incident has kept me going and pressing on doing what I'm now doing because I feel so strongly that God did actually speak those words to me.

There have been other times too, and I'm starting to try to trust that inner voice, the Holy Spirit, as the apostles did. The Bible records them as saying such things as "led by the Holy Spirit" or "it seemed good for them to do." So I'm not waiting for the big holy moments where I get all sweaty and nervous. I'm waiting for the simple moments of guidance and direction. This next example seems trivial, and it truly is, but I think there is no harm in starting with small things before stepping up to bigger ones.

I'm a huge Johnny Cash fan—anyone who knows me will tell you this. I had been wanting to buy his double-disc greatest hits record for some time and would even go to the store to buy it but walk out empty-handed. It was in stock, but something inside kept telling me to wait and not purchase it. I wasn't sure why, really, but like I said, I was and am trying to trust that I'm being guided by the Holy Spirit. So this goes on for at least two months, and then I'm in Nashville, and a friend randomly gives me the record I had been wanting to buy. Unopened even. This is just one small example, but I found it very encouraging. I have no shame in starting with such trivial matters.

But "Silence" is not about the moments when God speaks to us. It's about the moments when He doesn't, which seem to be most moments. I think the silence of God is one of the biggest arguments against Christianity. If He wants us to know He exists and communicates with us, then why doesn't He speak to us?

Instead, we often drift around almost aimlessly, feeling so distant, desiring just to hear a little something from God. Maybe not even words but something as trivial as making the toilet flush in the next room when we ask Him to. But maybe God is speaking to us all the time, only without words and on-demand, genie-like tricks. Through nature. Art. Music. Other people.

These things, I believe, have shown me the love, order, creativity, justice, mercy, and hope of God time and time again. Also through situations and circumstances that were too well placed to be mere chance.

I don't know why God so rarely chooses to speak to us with overwhelming assurance, when we are left with no doubt that He has just spoken. That's just the way He rolls though, and I have come to accept that difficult fact. When He isn't speaking, I believe Him to at least be listening. Worse than a talking God would be one that wouldn't listen. So I take comfort in knowing that when I sense Him to be so distant and uninvolved, He is at least listening to my every word.